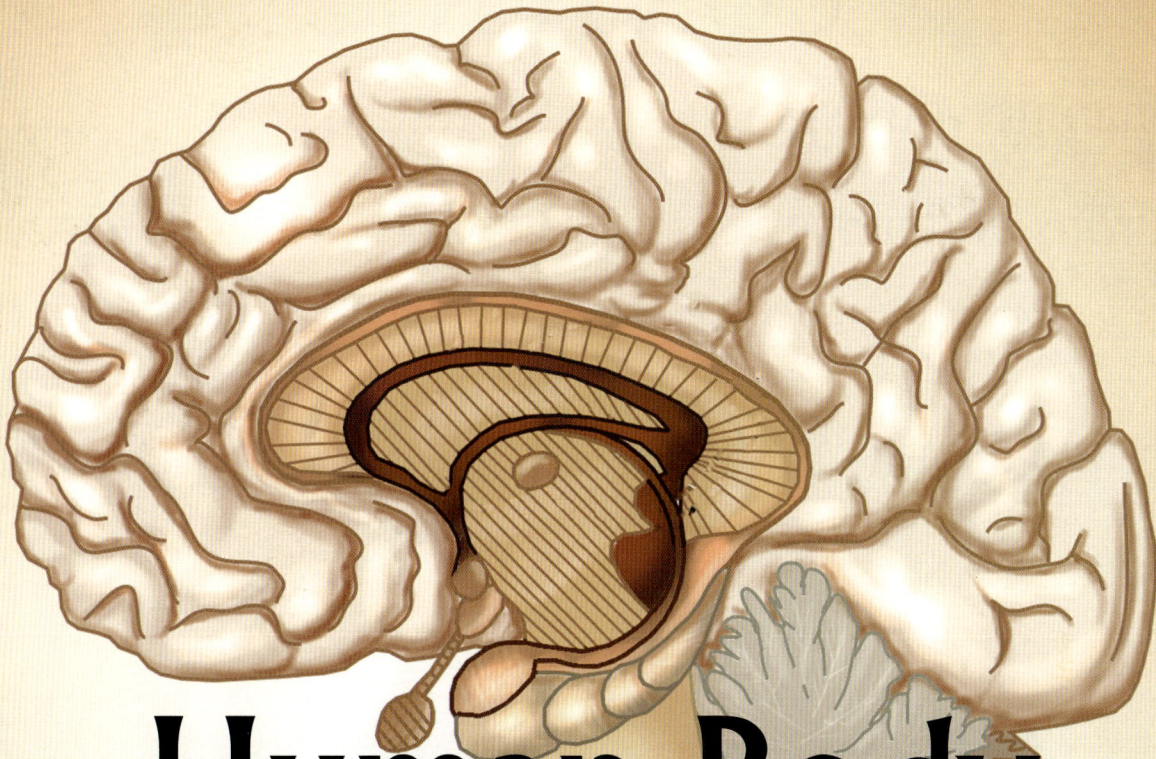

Human Body
NERVOUS SYSTEM

Edited by: Pallabi B. Tomar, Hitesh Iplani

Managing editor: Tapasi De

Designed by: Vijesh Chahal, Anil Kumar, Rohit Kumar

Illustrated by: Suman S. Roy, Tanoy Choudhury

Colouring done by: Vinay Kumar, Sonu, Kiran Kumari & Pradeep Kumar

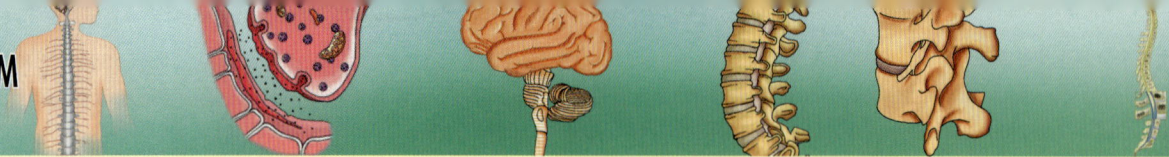

CONTENTS

Human nervous system 3

Neurons and nerves 6

Nerve 8

Central Nervous System 9

Brain 10

Spinal cord 13

Peripheral Nervous System 15

Diseases of the Nervous System 18

Healthy nerves 30

Test Your Memory... 31

Index.. 32

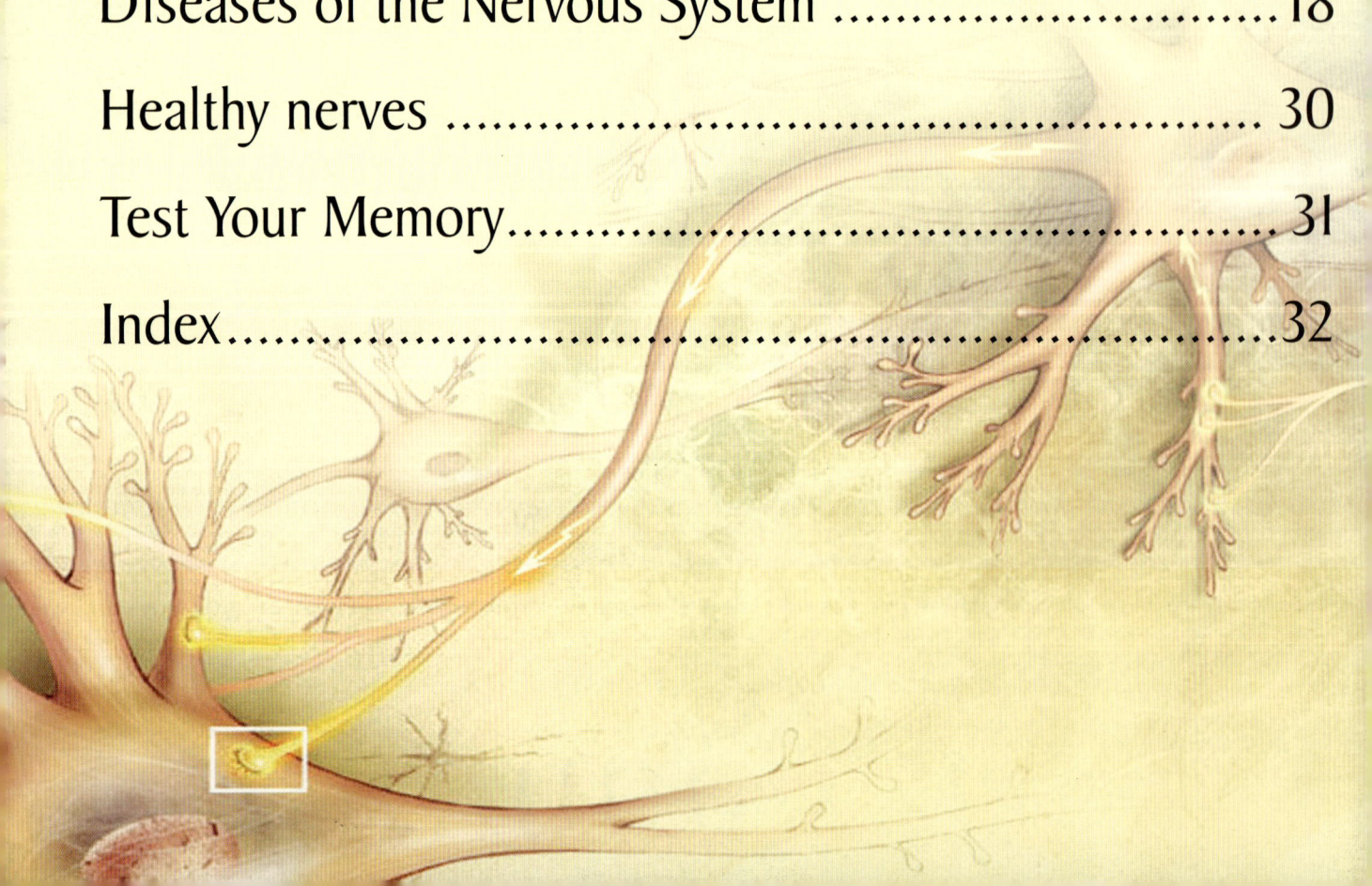

Human nervous system

Different organs of our body help us in doing various things like tasting, smelling, seeing, hearing, thinking, dreaming, singing, breathing, moving, running, laughing, remembering, feeling pain or pleasure, etc. Our nervous system allows us to perceive and understand all the activities our body does. It also helps us to control various movements, reactions and to form mental and physical responses to various situations.

Our nervous system consists of **brain**, **spinal cord** and an enormous network of **nerves** that run throughout our body. Our brain receives information about the external environment from nerves from various parts of the body and uses that information to direct all of our actions and reactions. The spinal cord runs from the brain down through the back and contains nerves that branch out to every organ and body part.

3

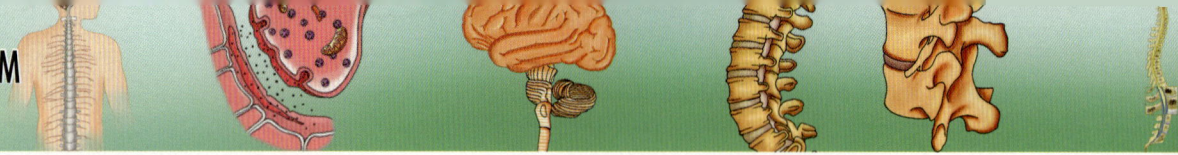

> **Nerves are cylindrical bundles of fibrous tissue that originate from the brain and divide again and again going to every part of our body.**

The smallest functional unit of the nervous system is a highly complex cell called **neuron** (say new-rons). Neurons join together to make nerves.

Nervous system is the control centre for our entire body. It is working every single second of the day exchanging millions of signals regarding feeling, thoughts and actions.

> **In human beings, having a complex nervous system allows us to process and understand language, abstract concepts, spread of cultures etc.**

To better understand how our nervous system functions think of the brain as a computer that controls our body and think of our nervous system as a network that spreads throughout our body. This network sends and receives messages from the brain to different parts of the body and vice-versa.

When the brain receives a message from anywhere in the body, the brain tells the body how to react. For example, if you accidentally touch a sharp object like a knife or a pin, the nerves in your skin fire off a message of pain to your brain. The brain then sends a message back telling the muscles in your hand to pull it away from the object. This whole process happens very fast and is completed in a very short amount of time, almost milliseconds!

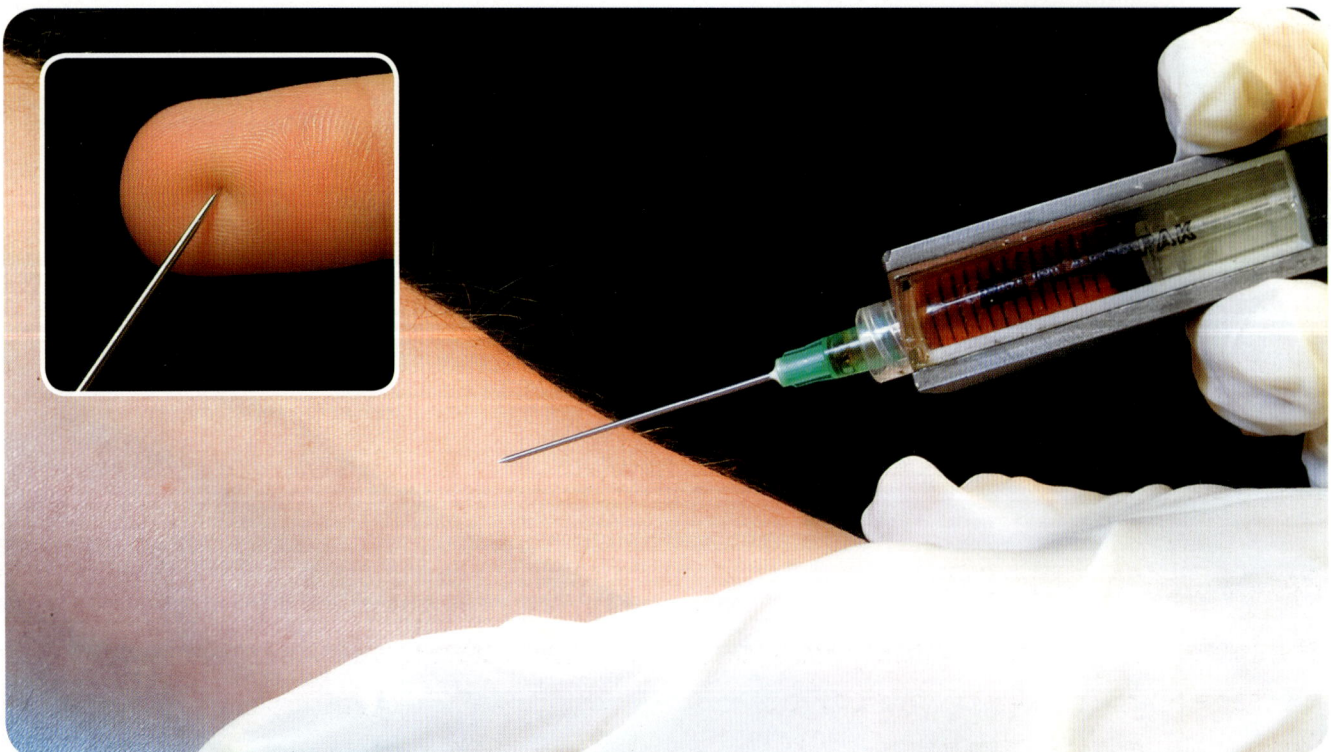

Functions of the nervous system

Basic functions of the nervous system are:

- To control the body and its various organs and coordinate its functions.

- It helps in analyzing and interpreting the information it receives.

- It stores previous experiences or memories which determine the course of action in future if faced with a similar situation again.

- It coordinates various functions of the internal organs of the body to maintain stability in the body fluids.

Parts of the nervous system

The human nervous system can be divided into two different parts:

1. **The Central Nervous System**

2. **The Peripheral Nervous System**

Central Nervous System

The **brain** and the **spinal cord** make up the Central Nervous System. The brain lies protected inside the skull and from there controls all the body functions by sending and receiving messages through the spinal cord.

Peripheral Nervous System

The peripheral nervous system carries messages back and forth between the Central Nervous System and the organs of the body. It sends information to the brain and carries orders from the brain to the organs involved.

The Peripheral System can be further divided into two different parts:

1. The **Somatic** Nervous System

2. The **Autonomic** Nervous System

The autonomic system is further divided into 2 parts:

1. The **Sympathetic** Nervous System

2. The **Parasympathetic** (para-sim-path-et-ik) Nervous System

These divisions of the nervous system will be discussed in the later chapters.

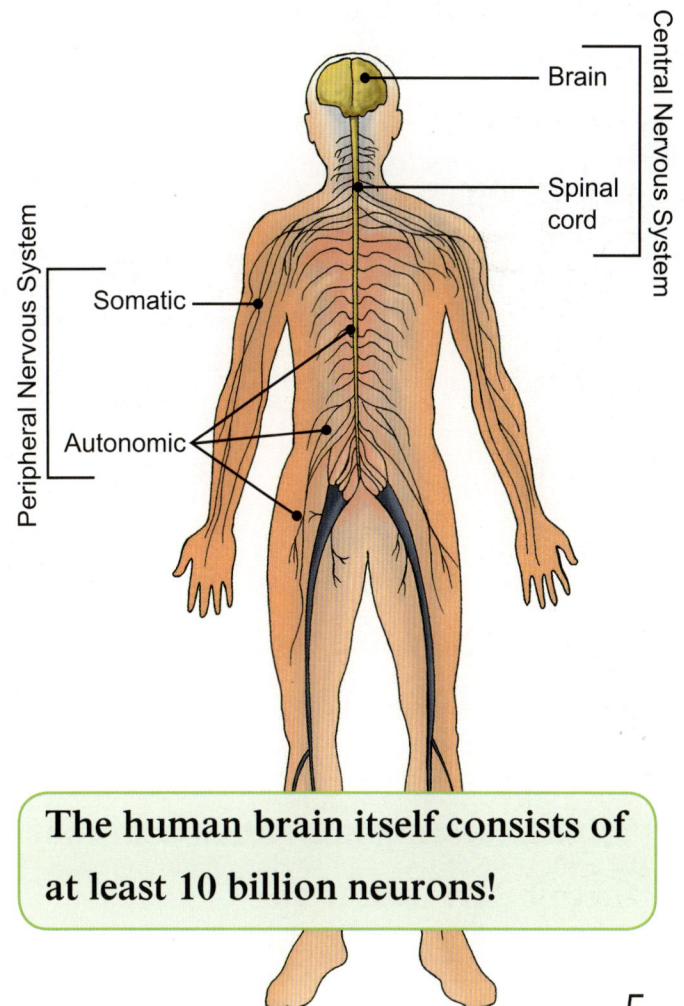

The human brain itself consists of at least 10 billion neurons!

5

Neurons and nerves

The nervous system is primarily made up of two categories of cells— **neurons** and **glial** cells. Parts of neurons combine to form **nerves**.

The nervous system is made up of millions and millions of highly specialised cells called neurons. They are the structural units of the nervous system. Each neuron has tiny branches that connect it to other neurons.

A neuron has three main parts— the **cell body**, **dendrites**, and an **axon**. Dendrites and axons both together form the nerve fibres.

Dendrites are hair-like threads branching off of the cell body like branches of a tree through which signals

from near-by neurons enter a particular neuron. Since each neuron contains many dendrites, a neuron can receive signals from many other surrounding neurons.

Astonishing fact

The human body contains about 200 billion neurons. Almost half of them are located in the brain.

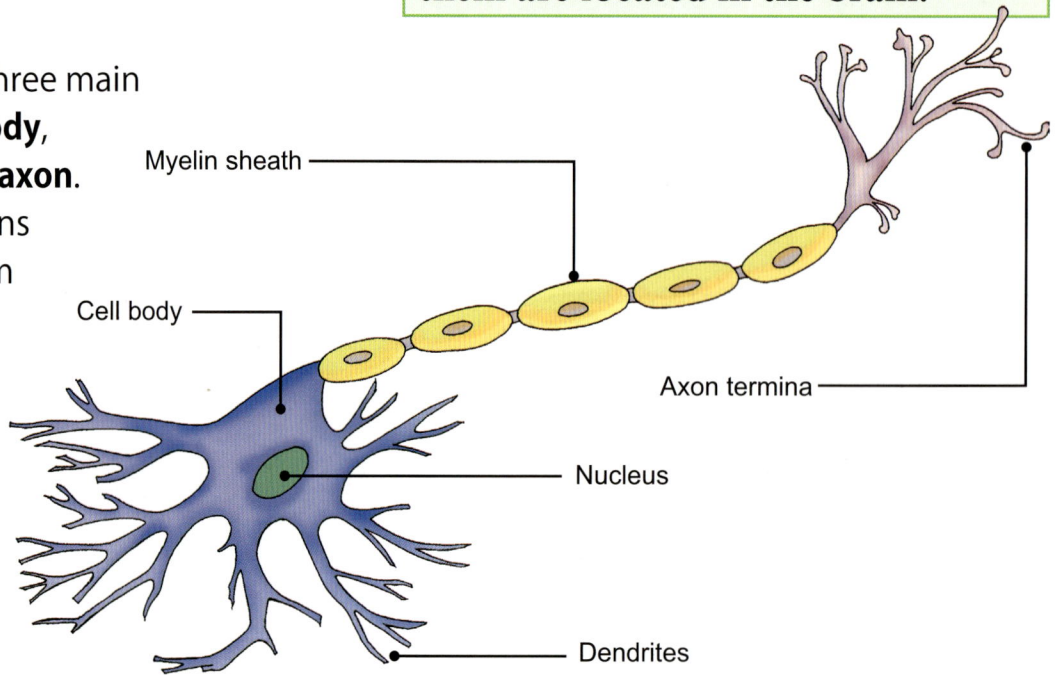

Myelin sheath

Cell body

Axon termina

Nucleus

Dendrites

When we are born, our brain has all the neurons it will ever have, but many of them are not connected to each other. When we learn things, the messages travel from one neuron to another, over and over. Gradually, our brain develops new connections (or pathways) between neurons. This helps in storing information so that things become easier and we can do them better next time.

Each neuron carries signals in only one direction. This prevents them from travelling both ways in a neuron and cancelling each other when they meet.

An **axon** is a tail-like structure that extends out of one end of a neuron. It ends in a cluster of branches called **axon terminals**. Axons perform the opposite function of dendrites— they carry messages away from the neuron.

Most long axons are covered by a white, fatty material called **myelin**. This covering is known as a **myelin sheath**. It serves to protect the axon and prevents messages travelling through it from getting lost.

Types of neurons

Neurons in our body may be divided into three categories— **sensory neurons**, **motor neurons**, and **interneurons**.

Sensory neurons: Also known as **afferent** neurons, these neurons carry impulses or sensations from receptors to the brain or spinal cord (Central Nervous System). Receptors are nerve endings that are located in the skin, skeletal muscles, joints, and internal organs and detect changes both inside and outside the body.

Motor neurons: Also known as **efferent neurons,** these neurons carry signals from the Central Nervous System to the cells in the peripheral system.

Both sensory and motor neurons make up the Peripheral Nervous System.

Interneurons: As their name implies, interneurons connect sensory and motor neurons. They work completely within the Central Nervous System.

Glial cells: Along with neurons, the nervous system contains other specialized cells called **glial** cells, which surround neurons in the Central Nervous System. They do not conduct impulses, but help to support and protect neurons, combining with them to form what is known as **nerve tissue**. They also supply neurons with nutrients and remove their wastes.

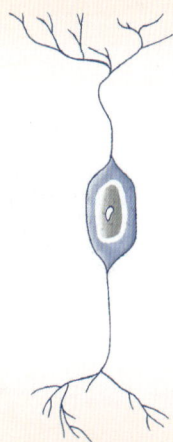

Bipolar
(Interneuron)

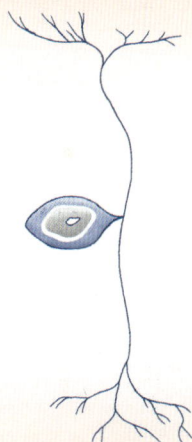

Unipolar
(Sensory Neuron)

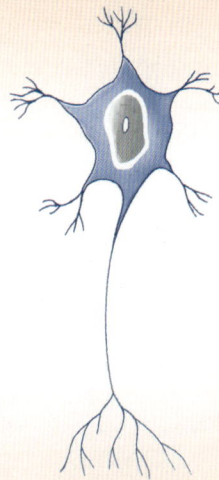

Multipolar
(Motoneuron)

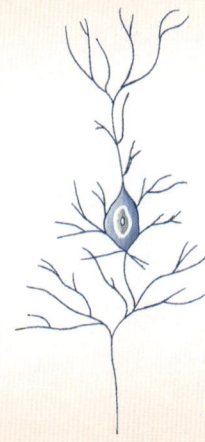

Pyrimidal
Cell

Types of neurons

7

Nerve

A nerve is a bundle of axons. Each axon or nerve fibre is wrapped in delicate connective tissue to form bundles. Finally, many bundles are bound together to form a nerve.

Sensory nerves send messages to the brain through the spinal cord. Motor nerves carry messages back from the brain to all the muscles and glands in our body. Mixed nerves contain axons of both sensory and motor neurons. The most abundant nerves, mixed nerves can conduct impulses both to and from the Central Nervous System.

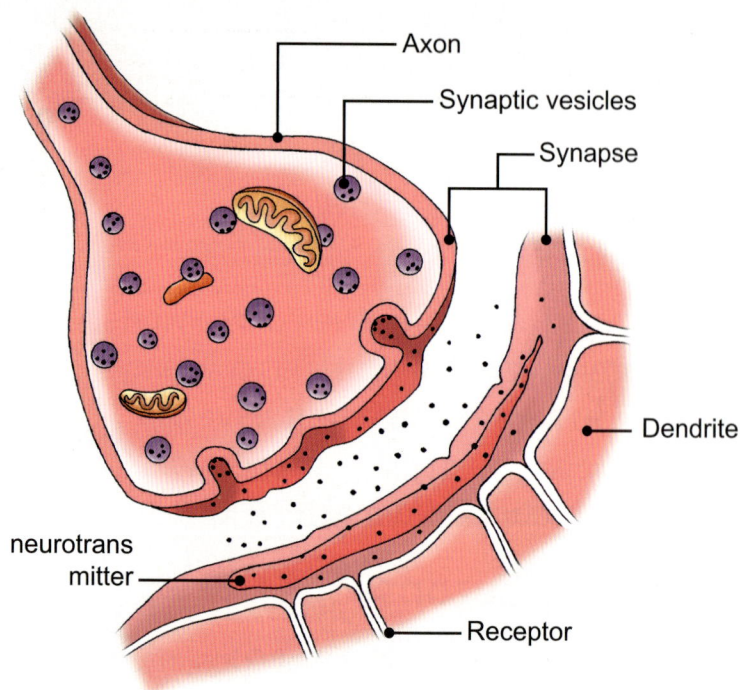

Axon

Synaptic vesicles

Synapse

Dendrite

neurotrans mitter

Receptor

How are messages passed?

When a neuron is alerted, by heat, cold, touch, sound vibrations or some other message, it generates a tiny electrical pulse. This electricity charge travels till the end of the neuron. At the end of each neuron there is a **synaptic terminal** which is full of extremely tiny sacs which hold

neurotransmitter chemicals. The electrical pulse in the cells triggers the release of chemicals that carry the pulse to the next cell. It functions like a relay of dominoes in which one falling domino trips the next one and so on.

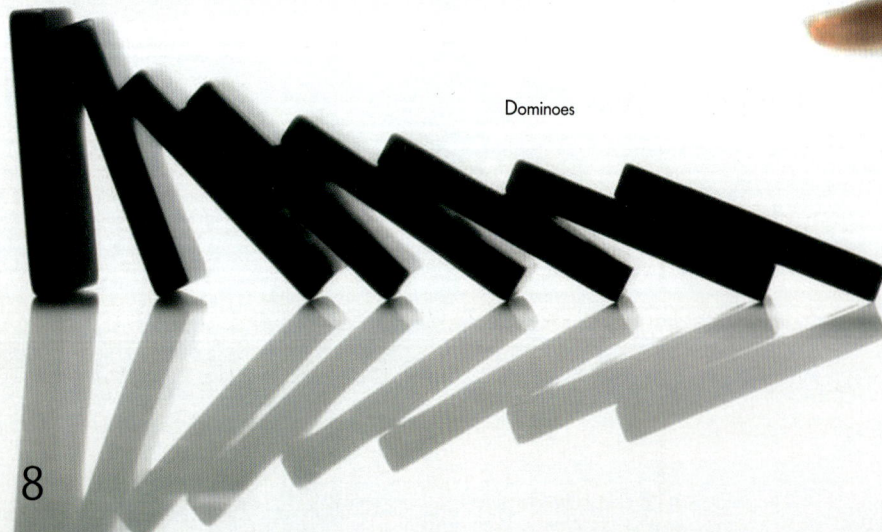

Dominoes

Central Nervous System

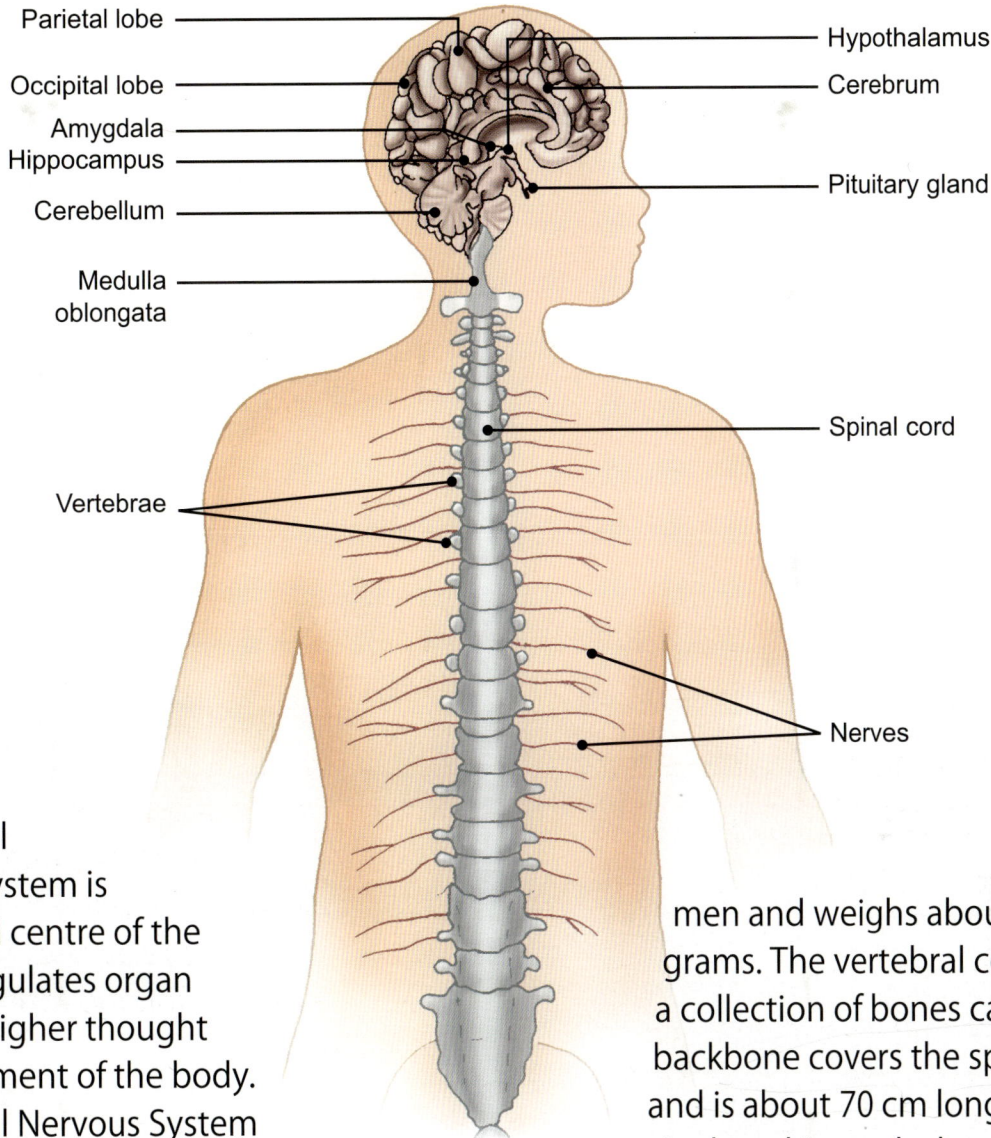

Parietal lobe

Occipital lobe

Amygdala

Hippocampus

Cerebellum

Medulla oblongata

Vertebrae

Hypothalamus

Cerebrum

Pituitary gland

Spinal cord

Nerves

The Central Nervous System is the control centre of the body. It regulates organ function, higher thought and movement of the body. The Central Nervous System is responsible for receiving and interpreting signals from the Peripheral Nervous System and also sends out signals to it, either consciously or unconsciously.

The Central Nervous System consists of the **brain** and **spinal cord**.

The spinal cord is about 43 cm long in adult women and 45 cm long in adult men and weighs about 35-40 grams. The vertebral column, a collection of bones called backbone covers the spinal cord and is about 70 cm long. The spinal cord is much shorter than the vertebral column.

Astonishing fact

The brain of an average adult human being weighs 1.3 to 1.4 kg. The brain contains about 100 billion neurons and trillions of glia cells!

9

Brain

The brain of the Central Nervous System is the organizing and processing centre. The human brain is highly compressed. Its many folds and grooves provide it with the additional surface area necessary for storing all of the body's important information.

It stores, organizes, retrieves and interprets information, controls our senses and regulates bodily functions, enables us to interact with people and things around us, and protects us from harm.

The brain performs number of tasks like:

- It controls body temperature, blood pressure, heart rate and breathing

- It accepts a huge amount of information about the world around us from our various senses such as seeing, hearing, smelling, tasting, touching, etc.

- It handles physical motion while walking, talking, standing or sitting

- It lets us think, dream, reason and experience emotions.

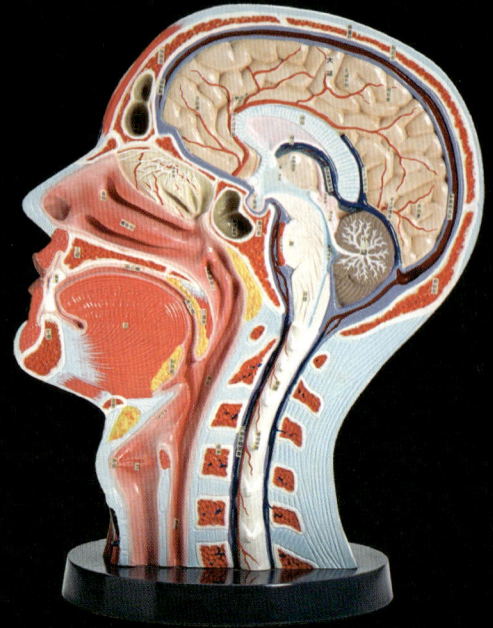

- Our brain also controls our emotions. They are controlled by little groups of cells on each side of the brain called the **amygdale**. The word 'amygdala' is Latin for almond and that is how this bunch of cells looks like

The brain receives signals from the spinal cord and from cranial nerves coming from and extending to the senses and to other organs.

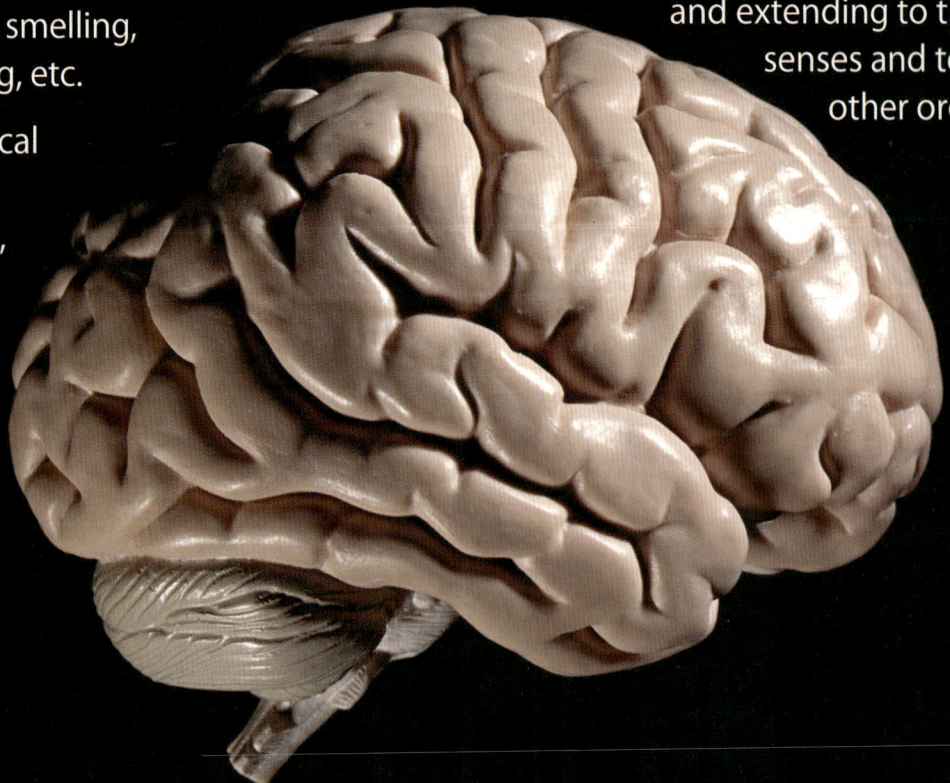

Parts of the brain

Our brain has many different parts that work together. Five of the most important parts of our brain are

1. **Cerebrum**

2. **Cerebellum**

3. **Brain stem**

4. **Pituitary gland**

5. **Hypothalamus**

The cerebrum is the biggest part of the brain. It makes up 85 per cent of the brain's weight. The cerebrum is the part of the brain responsible for thinking and controlling our voluntary muscles. Voluntary muscles are those muscles which we can move whenever we want to. The right half of the cerebrum controls the left side of our body and the left half controls the right side.

The **cerebrum** is divided into two halves, with one on either side of the head. The right half helps us in thinking about abstract things like music, colours, and shapes. The left half is analytical as it helps us in maths, logic, and speech. Our memory too is stored in the cerebrum.

The **cerebellum** is located at the back of the brain, below the cerebrum. It's quite smaller than the cerebrum. It controls balance, movement and coordination of our muscles. It helps in standing straight, maintaining balance, and moving around.

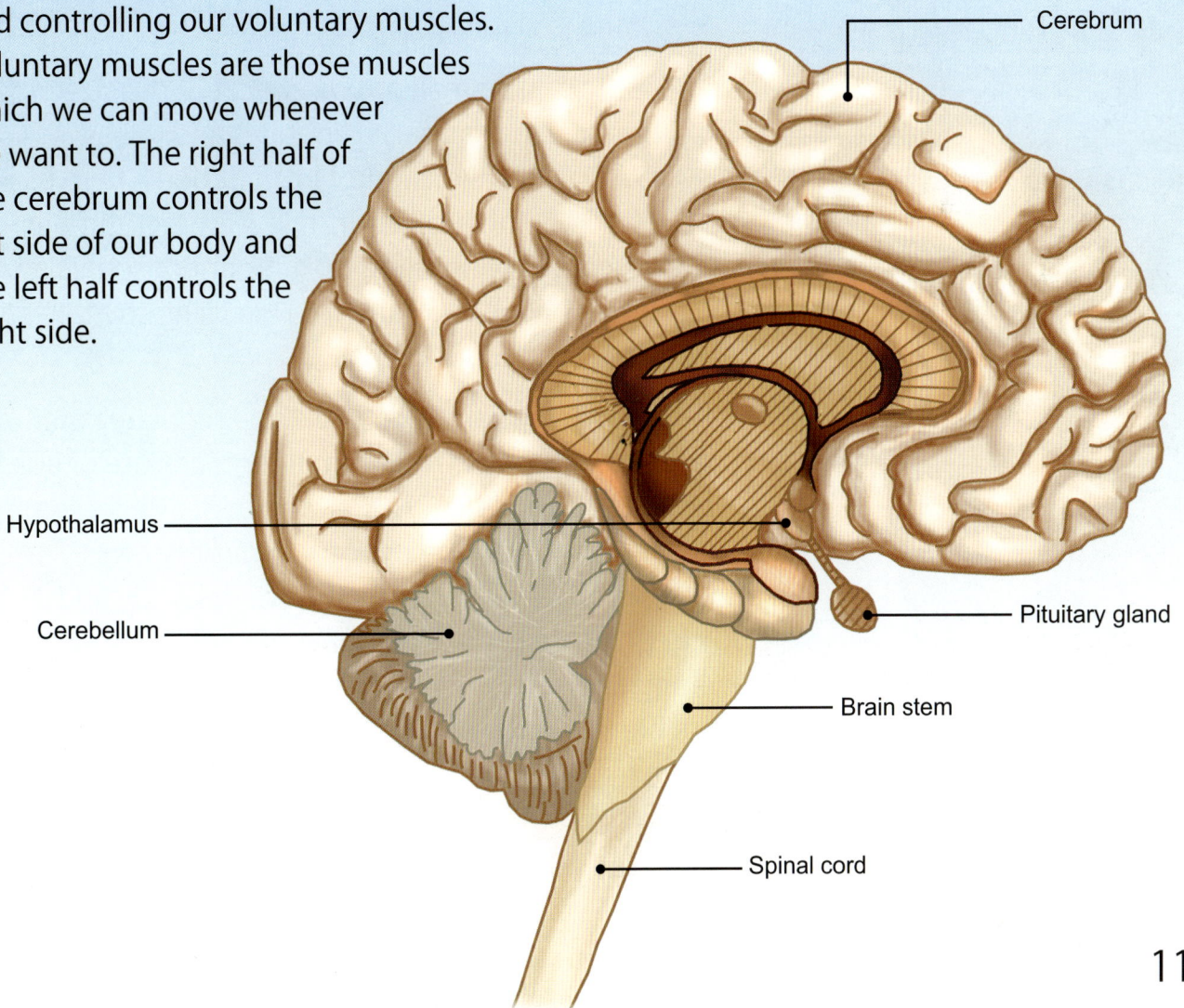

Cerebrum

Hypothalamus

Pituitary gland

Cerebellum

Brain stem

Spinal cord

11

Cerebrum

Midbrain

Brain stem

Pons

Medulla
oblongata

Cerebellum

Spinal cord

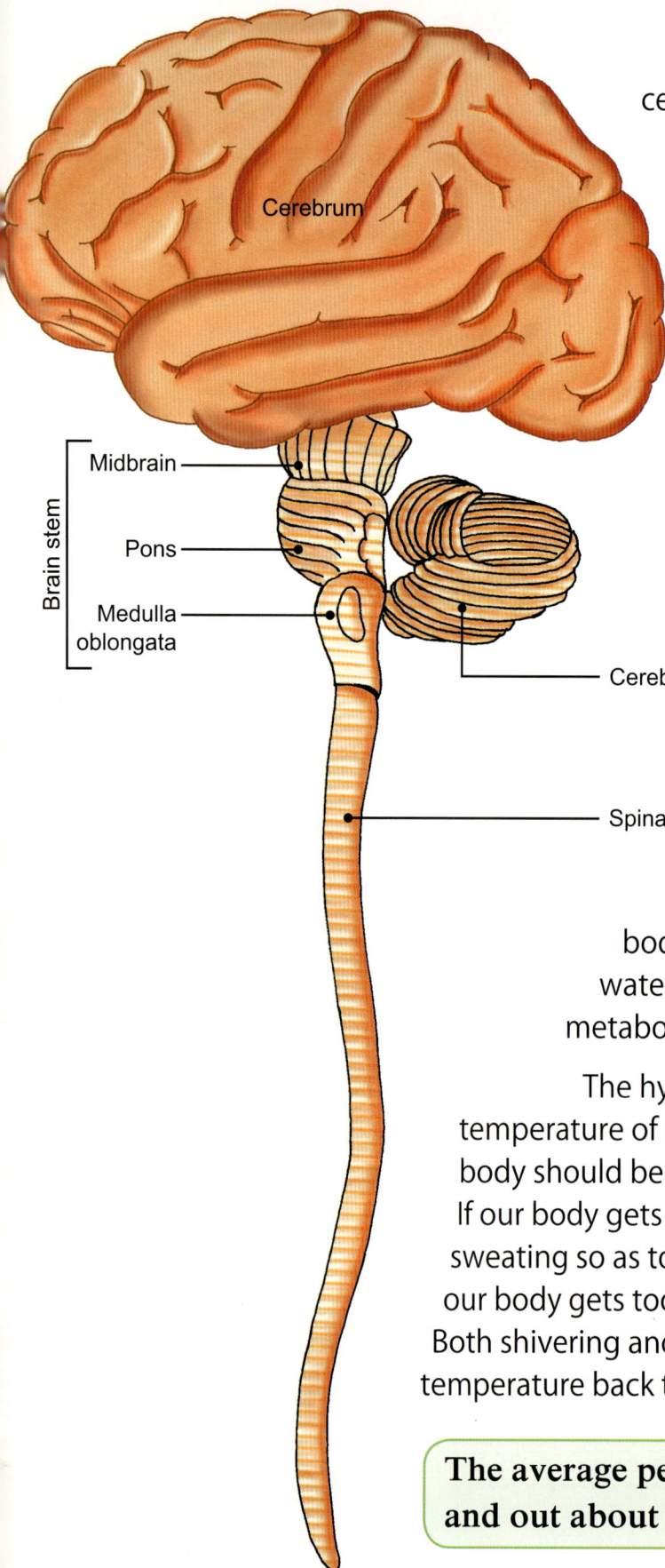

The brain stem is also located under the cerebrum and in front of the cerebellum. It connects the rest of the brain to the spinal cord. The brain stem controls functions like breathing air, digesting food, and circulating blood, in short all those functions which keep us alive.

The brain stem also controls our involuntary muscles which work automatically, without our commands. Some of the most important involuntary muscles are located in the heart and the stomach. The brain stem controls the pumping of more blood from our heart as and when required.

The pituitary gland is a very small organ, almost of the size of a pea. It produces and releases hormones into our body, help us in the growth and development of our body, in controlling the amount of sugars and water in our body and in controlling the rate of metabolism of our body.

The hypothalamus controls and regulates the temperature of our body. The normal temperature of our body should be about 98.6° Fahrenheit or 37° Celsius. If our body gets too hot, the hypothalamus enables sweating so as to release extra heat from the body and if our body gets too cold, the hypothalamus sets off shivering. Both shivering and sweating are attempts to get our body's temperature back to normal.

The average person at rest breathes in and out about 10-14 times per minute

Spinal cord

The spinal cord is a long, thin, tube-like bundle of nerve tissue extending from the lower part of the brain down through spine. All along the way various nerves branch out to the entire body forming the Peripheral Nervous System. It is protected by the bony vertebral column, also known as the **spinal column**.

Thirty-one pairs of **nerve roots** extend out along each side of the spinal cord. The nerve roots are bundles of axons belonging to sensory and motor neurons.

- Cerebrum
- Cerebellum
- Spinal column
- Spinal cord

Giraffes and humans have seven vertebrae in their necks.

The length of the spinal cord is much shorter than the length of the bony spinal column (vertebrae). The human spinal column is made up of 33 bones.

The spinal cord consists of a millions of nerve fibres which facilitate the transmission of electrical information between the brain and the various parts of the body. The size of the spinal cord is as big as the diameter of the human finger.

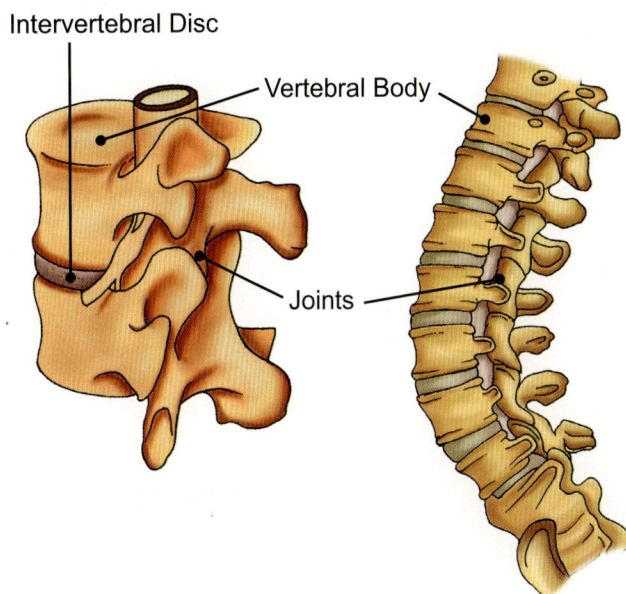

The first vertebra is also called the atlas. Atlas was one of the Titans (powerful Gods in Greek mythology). After a fight with Perseus (a Greek mythical hero), Atlas was turned to stone and had to carry the weight of the Earth and heavens on his shoulders. The first vertebra was named the Atlas since it carries the weight of the head.

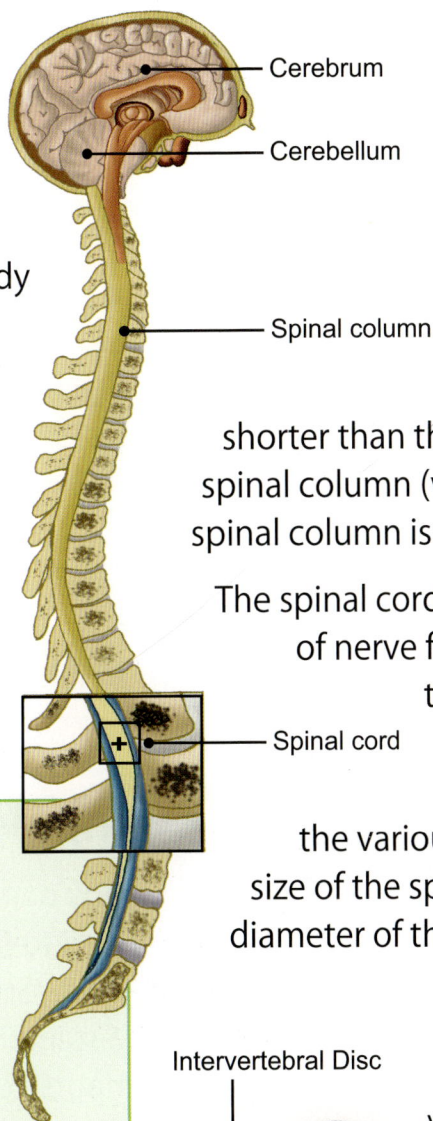

Intervertebral Disc

Vertebral Body

Joints

13

Functions of the spinal cord

Spinal cord is one of the most important parts of our body. It performs a number of functions:

1. Primarily, the spinal cord helps in connecting the various organs of human body to the brain. On one hand, it accepts the electrical information through sensory neurons and sends it to the brain. While on the other hand, it sends the signals from the motor area of the brain back to the various parts of the body.

2. Another function of the spinal cord is to coordinate various reflexes in our body. Reflexes are the built in responses of our body to a danger input. Some responses from our brain are required to travel at a greater speed. As a defence mechanism, the body reacts faster than the normal time it usually takes. This is known as a **reflex**.

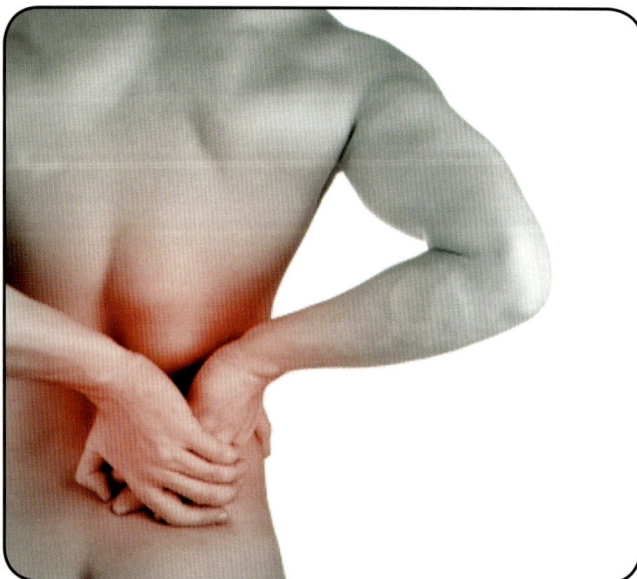

Injuries to the spinal cord

Any damage caused to the spinal cord can lead to failure of proper functioning of the body. Spinal cord injuries may range from a spinal shock lasting for about 24 to 48 hours, to further complications such as permanent paralysis.

Almost all important human body functions, including the respiratory control and sexual health, depend directly or indirectly on the spinal cord. Being one of the most important parts of our nervous system, the spinal cord has to be properly protected from any kind of damage. One should always wear safety gears and avoid putting oneself in a physically hazardous position.

Peripheral Nervous System

The Peripheral Nervous System runs from our spinal cord to other parts of our body like arms, legs, hands and feet. It comprises of nerves and neurons that send out information to and from the brain.

Peripheral Nervous System

Carnial nerves

Spinal nerves

The main function of the Peripheral Nervous System is to connect the Central Nervous System (brain and spinal cord) to the limbs and organs of our body. The Peripheral Nervous System is not protected by the bones of spine and skull.

The Peripheral Nervous System is divided into two parts called the **Somatic Nervous System** and the **Autonomic Nervous System**.

Somatic nervous system

The Somatic Nervous System is responsible for coordinating the body movements, and also for receiving signals from the external environment. It regulates activities that are under conscious control. This system controls the skeletal muscles of our body.

The senses of touch, taste, sight, sound and smell are controlled by the Somatic Nervous System. Also, the Somatic Nervous System enables our body to feel heat, cold and pain. It also controls involuntary actions such as blinking.

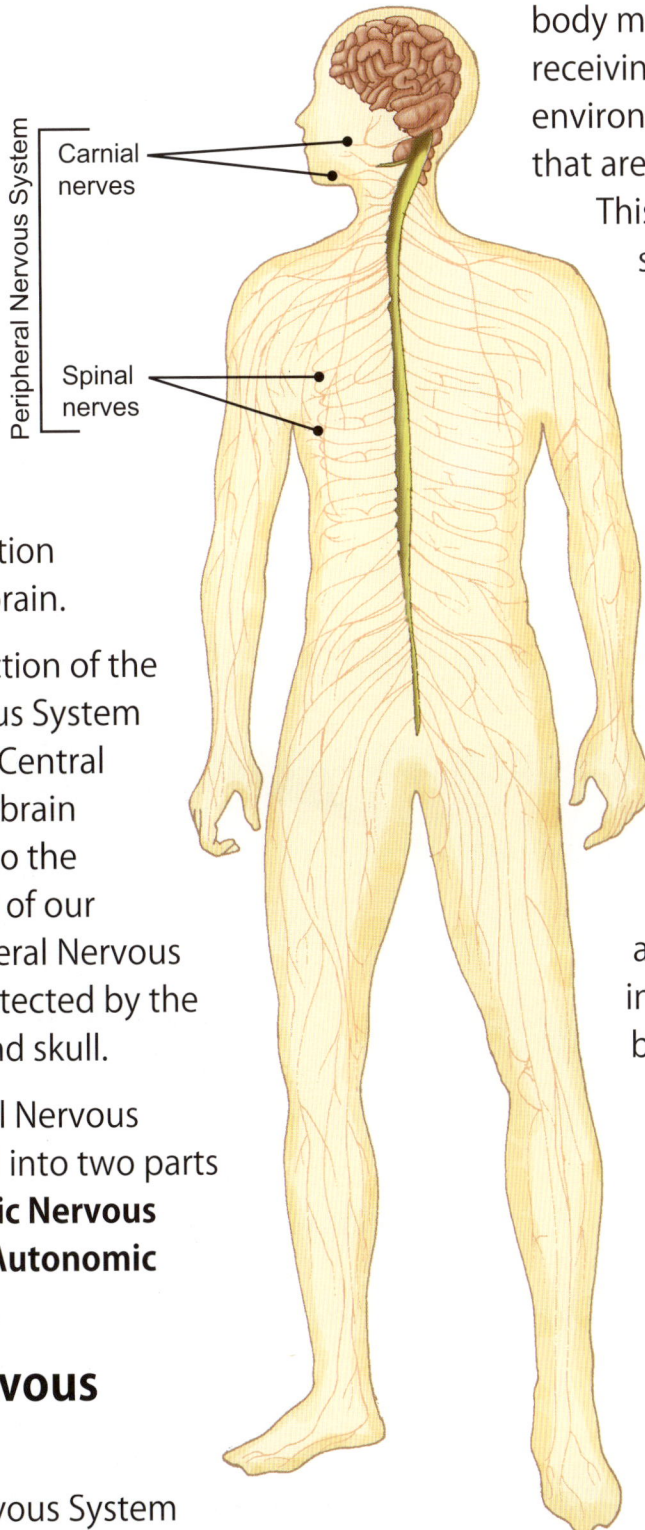

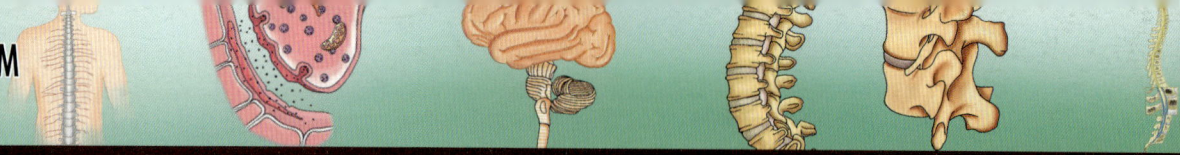

Autonomic Nervous System

The second part of the peripheral nervous system is the autonomic nervous system. The autonomic system controls and regulates the body internally. It regulates the function of glands such as salivary, gastric, sweat and adrenal glands.

Autonomic nervous system is in control when the body is at rest. It regulates processes such as increased and decreased heart rates as a response to a situation, secretion of digestive fluids and the body's reaction to stress.

It controls involuntary muscles, such the muscles of the heart which work on their own and we do not have to think about them to make them work. Therefore, this system is also called the **Involuntary Nervous System**.

The autonomic nervous system has been divided into two further parts:

1. **Sympathetic Nervous System**
2. **Parasympathetic Nervous System**

Astonishing fact

The fastest nerve signals travel at speeds that exceed 100 m per second!

Body at rest

Sympathetic Nervous System

The **Sympathetic Nervous System** responds to dangerous and scary situations by increasing heartbeat and blood pressure. The sense of excitement one feels an adventurous or thrilling situation is also generated by the Sympathetic Nervous System.

Nerves of the sympathetic division speed up heart rate, widen our pupils, relaxes the bladder, raises blood pressure, causes erection of hairs on our body (gooseflesh) and secretion of small quantities of thick saliva. The Sympathetic Nervous System is also involved in the **flight or fight response**. This is a response to potential danger that results in accelerated heart rate and rest of the activities described above. These activities

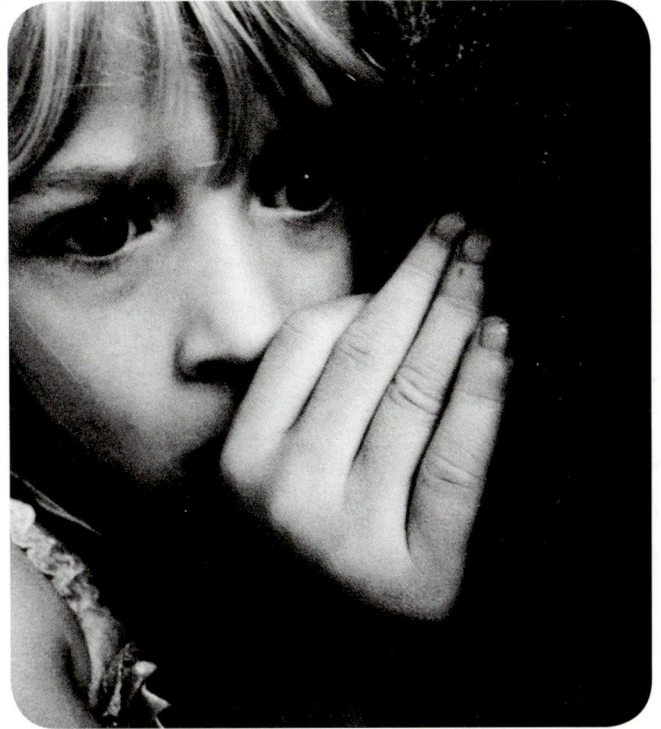

Frightened

occur in emergencies such as fright and are associated with the expenditure of energy as a response to the need to flee, fight or be frightened.

Parasympathetic Nervous System

The **Parasympathetic Nervous System** controls various functions which include slowing the heart rate, constricting pupils, and contracting the bladder. As we can see, this system controls the activities which control the energy expenditure. The Parasympathetic Nervous System calms the body therefore it is also known as the **wine and dine** nervous system.

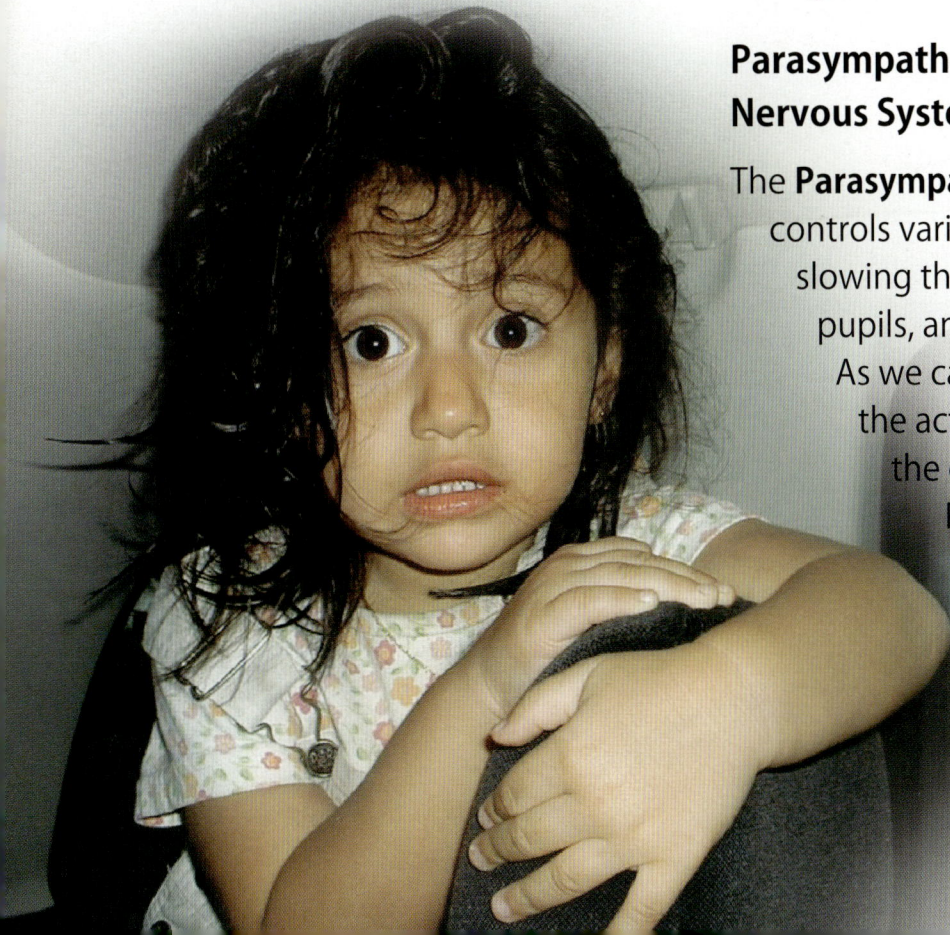

17

Diseases of the nervous system

Trauma or injury to the spinal cord or brain can affect both the peripheral nervous system and the Central Nervous System. Damage to the Central Nervous System is often more serious than damage to the Peripheral Nervous System. Some of the diseases of the nervous system are:

Cerebral palsy

It is a disorder of movement resulting from damage to the brain before, during or immediately after birth.

Causes

It is often associated with other neurological and mental problems. There are many causes including birth injury, hypoxia (oxygen deficiency during birth), jaundice and infection.

A neurologist is a doctor who specializes in treating diseases or disorders affecting the nervous system.

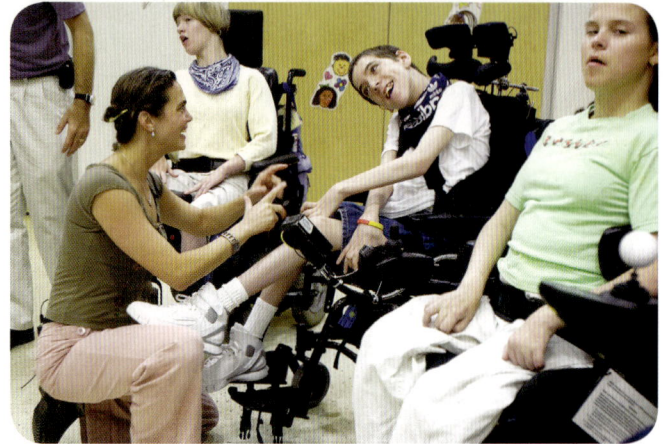

Symptoms/ effects

The most common disability is **spastic paralysis**.

Sensation is often affected, leading to a lack of balance and intelligence, posture and speech are frequently affected.

Other features include epilepsy, visual impairment, squint, reduced hearing, and behavioural problems.

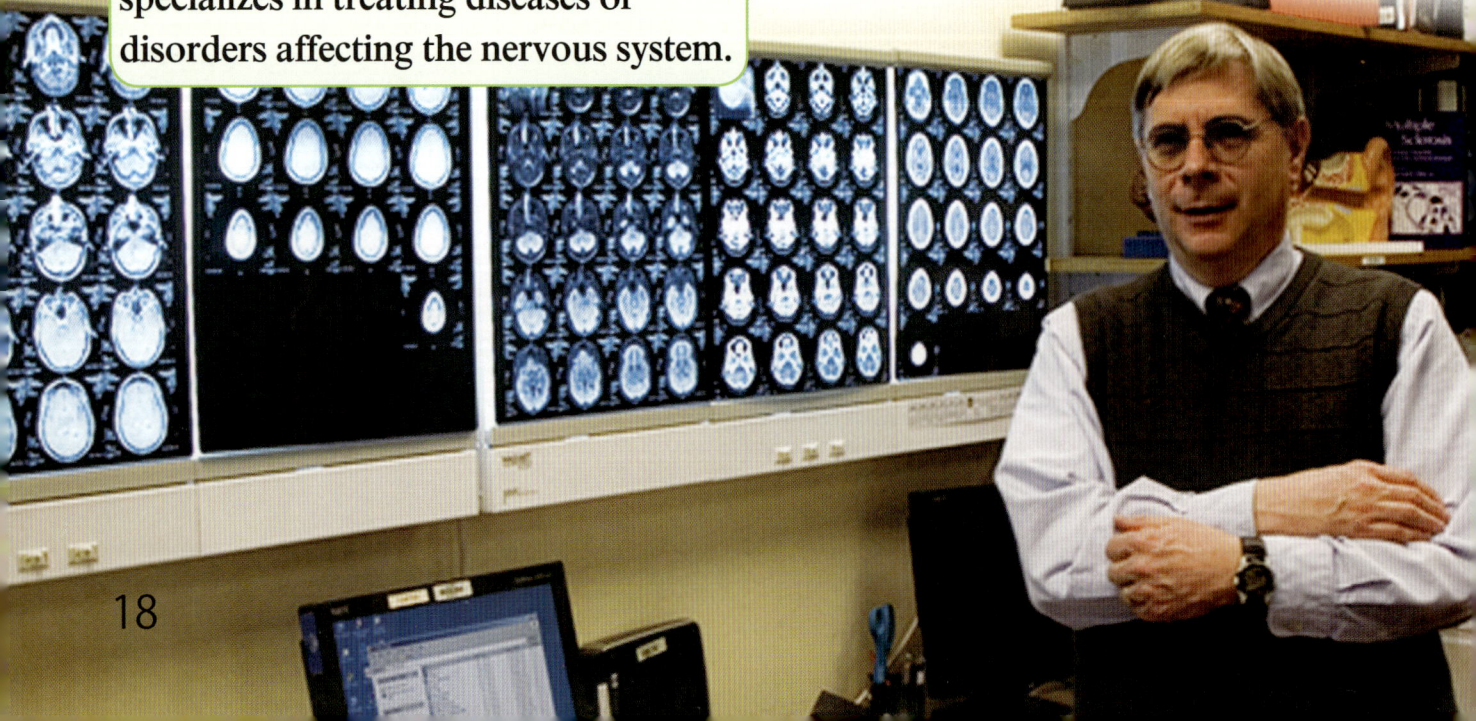

Multiple Sclerosis

Multiple sclerosis (MS) is a chronic disease of the Central Nervous System affecting young and middle-aged adults. In MS, the communication between the brain and other parts of the body becomes disrupted. Some individuals with MS may be mildly affected while others may lose their ability to write, speak or walk.

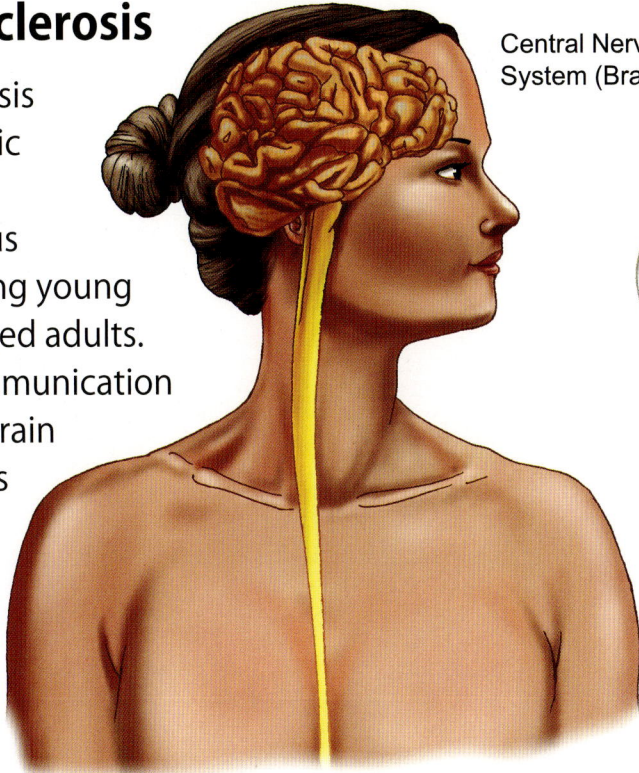

Central Nervous System (Brain and

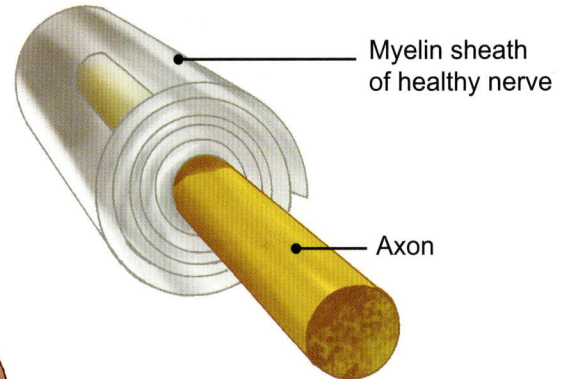

Myelin sheath of healthy nerve

Axon

In multiple sclerosis the myelin sheath, which is a covering that wraps around the axon is destroyed with inflammation and scarring

Causes

This is caused by destruction of **myelin**, the fatty covering that insulates nerve cell fibres in the brain and spinal cord to assist the high-speed transmission of electrochemical messages between the brain, the spinal cord, and the rest of the body. When myelin is damaged, transmission of messages may be slowed or blocked completely. The underlying cause of the nerve damage remains unknown.

There are many possible causes of MS, including:

- Viruses

- Environmental factors

- Genetic factors

- Immune system factors

Symptoms and effects

Multiple sclerosis can have the following symptoms:

- Unsteady gait and shaky movement of the limbs

- Rapid involuntary movements of the eyes

- Defects in speech pronunciation

19

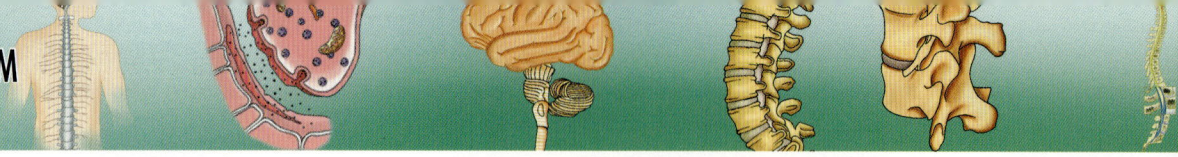

Parkinson's disease

Parkinson's disease is a slowly progressing, chronic (lasts over a long period of time) disease that gradually affects the nervous system. Although the disease may appear in younger patients, it usually affects people in late middle age. It is not contagious, nor is it likely passed on from generation to generation.

Causes

Parkinson's disease can be a result of deficiency of the dopamine. Dopamine is a neurotransmitter chemical found in the brain which is essential for the normal functioning of the Central Nervous System. It can also be triggered by the process of aging. The particular cause of PD is unknown.

Symptoms and effects

The following symptoms and effects of the disease have been observed in the patient:

* Tremor, rigidity in movements
* Trembling of the arms, jaw, legs, and face
* Stiffness or rigidity of the limbs
* Slow movement
* Impaired balance and coordination
* Expressionless face
* Unmodulated voice (voice with no variations in the pitch)
* An increasing tendency to stoop
* A shuffling walk

Bell's Palsy

Bell's palsy involves paralysis of the facial nerve causing weakness of the muscles of one side of the face and an inability to close the eye. It begins suddenly and worsens over three to five days. This condition may be accompanied by pain or discomfort on one side of the face and head.

> **Bell's Palsy was named after Sir Charles Bell, a Scottish surgeon and physiologist, for his work on facial palsy. In 1821, he demonstrated that the facial nerve was a separate nerve.**

It affects men and woman equally, usually between the ages of 15 and 60.

Causes

A particular cause of Bell's palsy is unknown, however, it has been suggested that the disorder may come from one's parents. It also may be related to the following:

- Diabetes
- High blood pressure
- Trauma
- Toxins
- Infection

Symptoms and effects

The following are the most common symptoms of Bell's palsy. However, symptoms may differ in different individuals. Symptoms may include:

- Disordered movement of the muscles that control facial expressions such as smiling, squinting, blinking, or closing the eyelid
- Loss of feeling in the face
- Headache
- Tearing
- Drooling
- Loss of the sense of taste on the front of the tongue
- Excessive sensitivity to sound in the affected ear
- Inability to close the eye on the affected side of the face

The symptoms of Bell's palsy might resemble other medical problems. It is wise to consult a doctor for a diagnosis.

The treatment for Bell's palsy is to protect the patient's eyes from drying during the night. The use of eye drops during the day and ointment at bedtime helps to protect the cornea of the eye. Most of the people with Bell's palsy recover full facial strength and expression, usually over weeks to months.

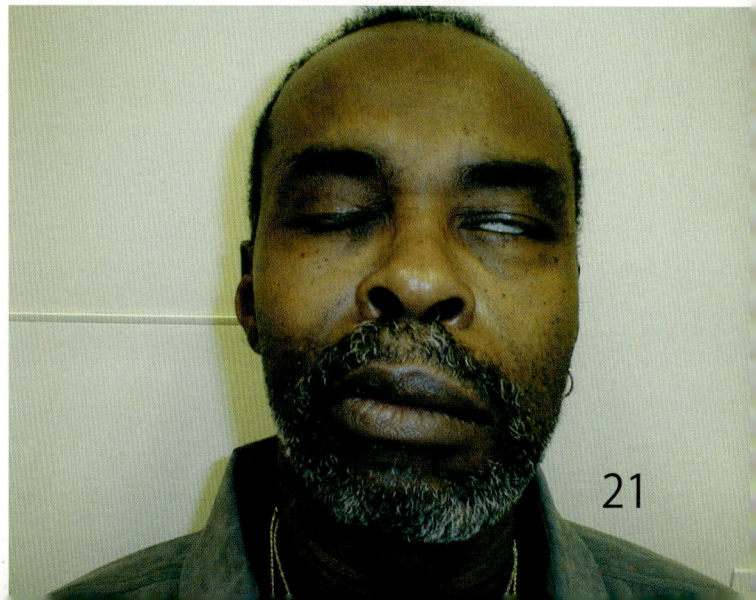

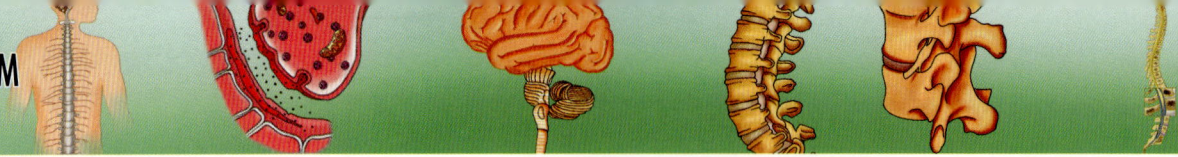

Alzheimer's disease

A patient of the **Alzheimer's disease** experiences the following:

- Impaired memory, thinking, and behaviour
- Confusion
- Restlessness
- Personality and behaviour changes
- Impaired judgment
- Impaired communication
- Inability to follow directions
- Language deterioration
- Impaired visual-spatial skills

It is a slowly progressing disease that affects the brain.

Causes

The causes of Alzheimer's disease have still not been entirely understood despite intense scientific investigation. Suspected causes often include the following:

- Age and family history
- Certain genes
- Abnormal protein deposits in the brain
- Other risk and environmental factors

Symptoms

The following are the most common symptoms of Alzheimer's disease. However, each individual may experience symptoms differently. Symptoms may include:

- Memory loss that affects working capabilities
- Difficulty in doing familiar tasks
- Problems with language
- Confusion regarding time and place
- Poor or decreased judgment
- Problems with abstract thinking
- Misplacing things
- Changes in mood or behaviour
- Changes in personality
- Loss of initiative

At present, there is no cure available for Alzheimer's disease. However, the research for a cure is on. Medical help for some of the most troubling symptoms of Alzheimer's disease like depression, behavioural disturbance, sleeplessness, etc. is however available.

Helping an Alzheimer's patient

The treatment program for persons with Alzheimer's differs depending upon the symptoms, expression and progression of the disease. With Alzheimer's treatment, it is important to remember that, any skills lost will not be regained. The following considerations must be kept in mind:

- Physical exercise, proper nutrition and social activities are important
- Daily activities should be planned

- As normal functioning is lost, activities and daily routines should be planned in such a way so as to allow the individual to participate as much as possible

- Allow the individual to complete as many things by himself/herself as possible after providing an initiative

- Label drawers/cabinets/closets according to their contents to provide hints for desired behaviour

- Keep the individual safe by removing various safety hazards such as pointed objects which can cause harm

Seizures

What is a seizure?

A seizure happens when part(s) of the brain receives a burst of large amount of electrical signals that interrupt normal brain function for some time. There are several different types of seizures like:

1. Partial seizures

Partial seizures take place when abnormal electrical brain function occurs in one or more areas of one side of the brain. The person may experience an **aura** before the seizure occurs. An aura is a strange feeling, either consisting of visual changes, hearing abnormalities or changes in the sense of smell. Two types of partial seizures include the following:

- **Simple partial seizures**: These seizures typically last less than one minute.

Screaming

Laughing

- **Complex partial seizures**: This type of seizure usually lasts between one to two minutes. Consciousness is usually lost during these seizures and a variety of behaviours can occur. These behaviours may range from gagging, lip smacking, running, screaming, crying or laughing. When the person regains consciousness, the person may complain of being tired or sleepy after the seizure.

Crying

2. Generalized seizures

Generalized seizures involve both sides of the brain. There is loss of consciousness. Types of generalized seizures include the following:

• **Absence seizures (petit mal seizures)**: These seizures are characterized by an altered state of consciousness and staring episodes. Typically, the person's posture is maintained during the seizure. The mouth or face may move or the eyes may blink. The seizure usually lasts no longer than 30 seconds. When the seizure is over, the person may not recall what had just occurred and may go on with his/her activities, acting as though nothing happened. These seizures may occur several times a day.

• **Atonic seizures**: With atonic seizures the person may fall from a standing position or suddenly drop his/her head. During the seizure, the person is unresponsive.

• **Generalized tonic-clonic seizures (or grand mal seizures)**: This seizure is

Fatigue

Sudden fall

characterized by five distinct phases that occur. The body, arms, and legs will contract, extend and shake, followed by a contraction and relaxation of the muscles. After that the person may be sleepy, have problems with vision or speech, and may have a bad headache, fatigue, or body aches.

Causes

The exact cause of a seizure is not known. Some of the common seizures are caused by the following:

- Alcohol or drugs
- Head trauma
- Infection
- Brain tumour
- Neurological problems
- Drug withdrawal
- Medications

Symptoms

The person may have varying degrees of symptoms depending upon the type of seizure. The following are warning signs of seizures:

- Falling suddenly for no apparent reason
- Not responding to noise or words for brief periods
- Appearing confused or in a haze
- Sleepiness and irritable upon waking in the morning

Staring

- Nodding the head
- Periods of rapid eye blinking
- Staring
- Jerking movements of the arms and legs
- Stiffening of the body
- Loss of consciousness
- Breathing problems or breathing stops
- Loss of bowel or bladder control

During the seizure, the person's lips may become bluish and breathing may not be normal. The movements are often followed by a period of sleep, fatigue or confusion.

How to help

To see a person having a seizure for the first time can be scary, especially if one does not know what to do. With some seizure types little first aid may be needed.

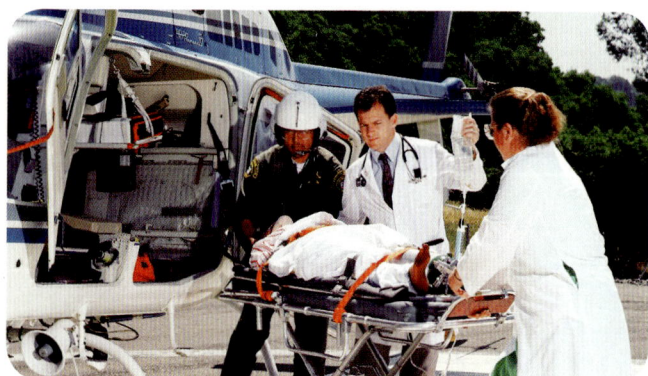

DON'T

- Restrain the person's movements
- Put anything in the person's mouth
- Try to move them unless they are in danger
- Give them anything to eat or drink until they are fully recovered

Call ambulance if...

- The seizure continues for more than five minutes

DOS

- Protect the person from injury; remove any sharp or hard objects lying nearby.
- Guide the person away from danger if she/he is having a partial seizure.
- Cushion the persons head if they fall down.
- When the seizure is at an end, place the person in the recovery position. This will help in breathing.
- Stay with the person until she/he has regained full consciousness.
- Go over any missed events.

- One tonic-clonic seizure follows another without the person regaining consciousness between seizures
- The person is injured during the seizure
- You believe the person needs urgent medical attention

Epilepsy

Epilepsy is a condition in which a person experiences long-term seizures in the person. Epilepsy seizures are seizures that occur more than once and without a particular cause. These seizures are also called idiopathic seizures.

Causes

The exact cause of epilepsy is not known. It maybe caused by the following:

- Family history
- Genetic problem
- Underlying brain problem

Recovery position

Recovery position is one in which a person who has just experienced a seizure must be positioned into so as to promote breathing and prevent choking. These steps should be followed once the jerking has stopped.

1. Bend down on the floor to one side of the person.

2. Place the person's arm that is nearest to you at a right angle to her body so that it is bent at the elbow with the hand pointing upwards.

27

3

3. Gently pick up her other hand with your palm against her. Now place the back of her hand onto their opposite cheek (for example, against her left cheek if it is their right hand). Keep your hand there to guide and support her head as you roll her.

4. Now use your other arm to reach across to the person's knee that is furthest from you and pull it up so that her leg is bent and other foot is flat on the floor.

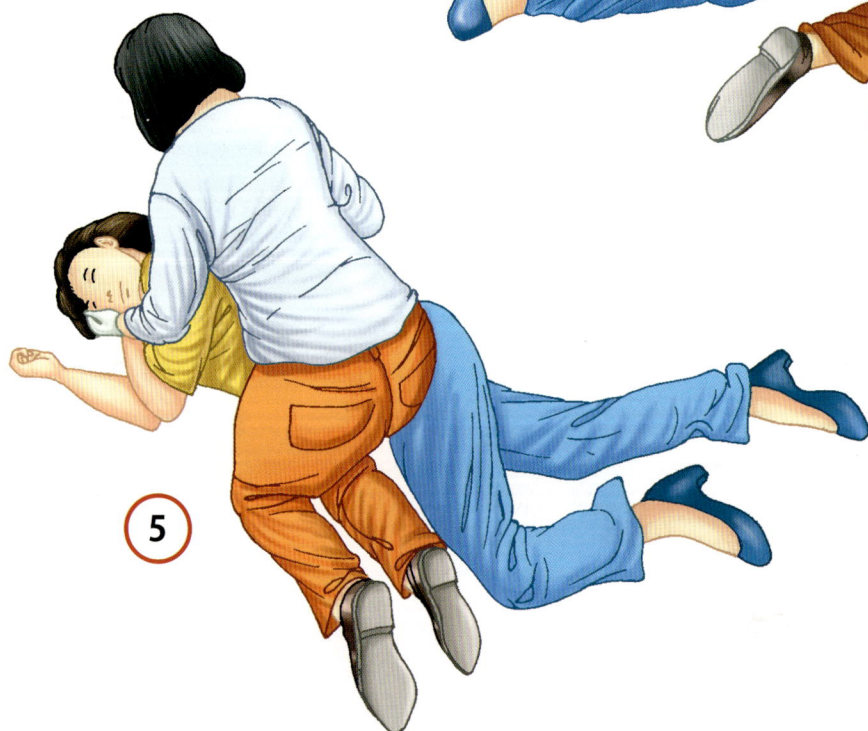

4

5

5. Now, with your hand still on the person's knee, pull her knee towards you so that she rolls over onto her side, facing you.

6. Move the bent leg that is nearest to you, away from her body so that it rests on the floor.

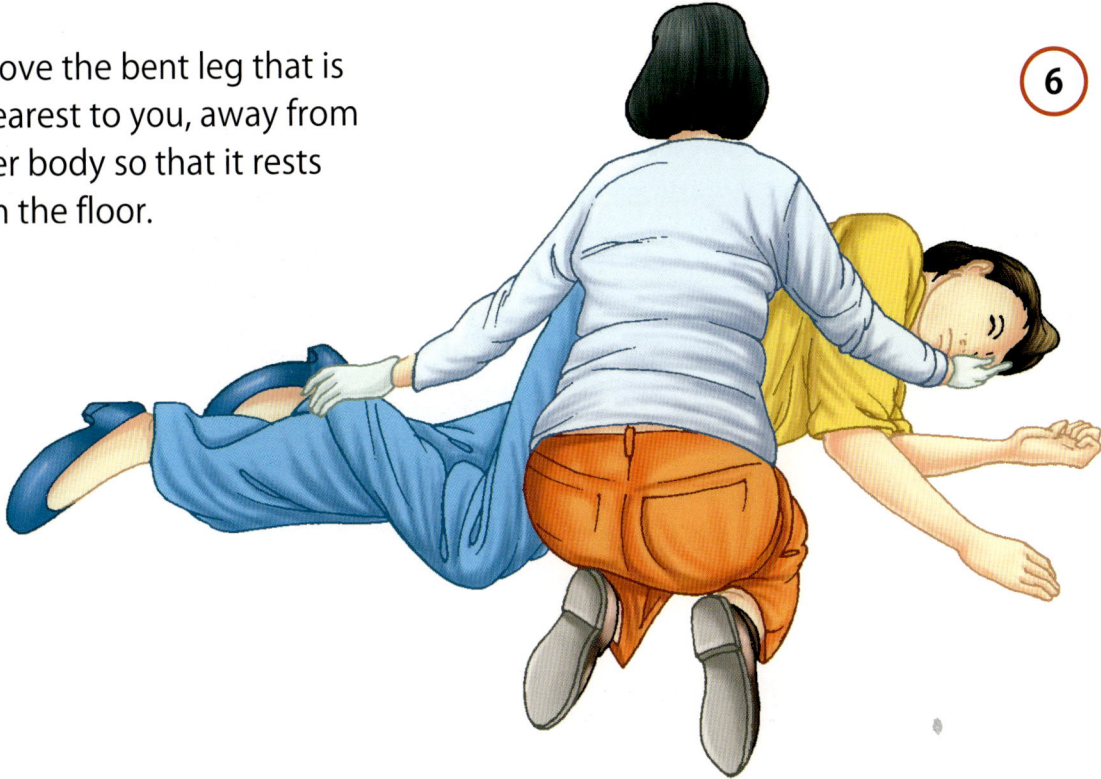

7. Lastly, gently raise her chin to tilt her head back slightly, as this will open up her airway and help her to breathe. Check that nothing is blocked in her airway. If there is an obstruction, remove this if you can. Stay with the person making him/her comfortable until they have fully recovered.

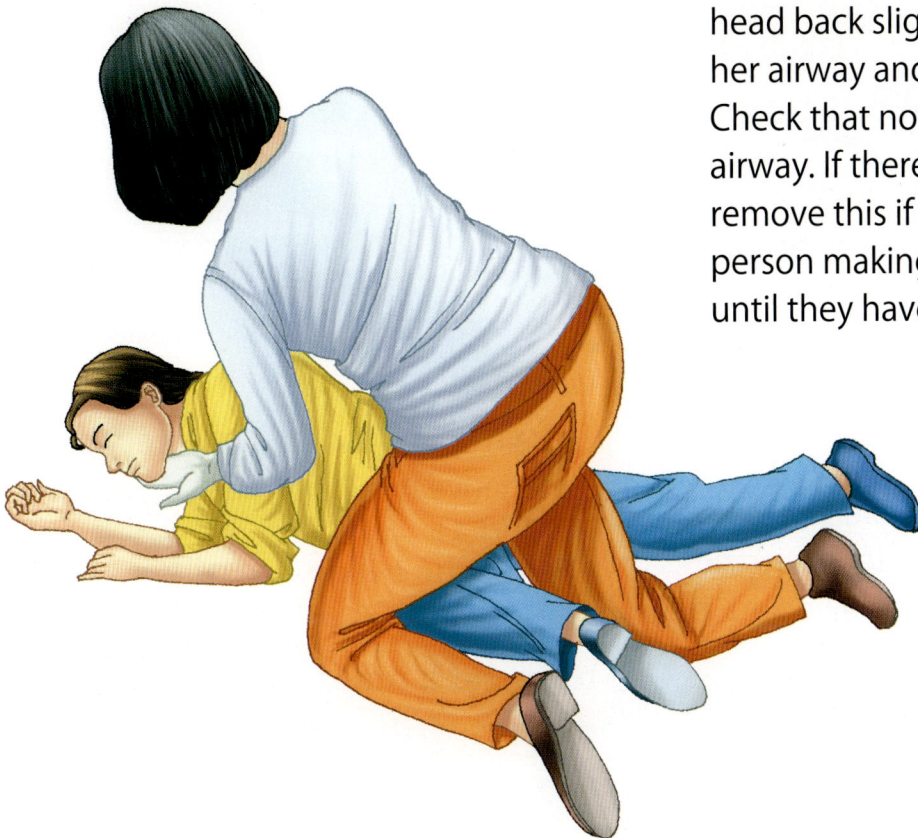

Healthy nerves

There are several things that you can do to promote nervous system's health and these include:

1. Eat a healthy diet rich in potassium and calcium, two minerals that are important for the nervous system

2. Exercise regularly

3. Wear a helmet while riding a bike or during other activities that require protection for the head

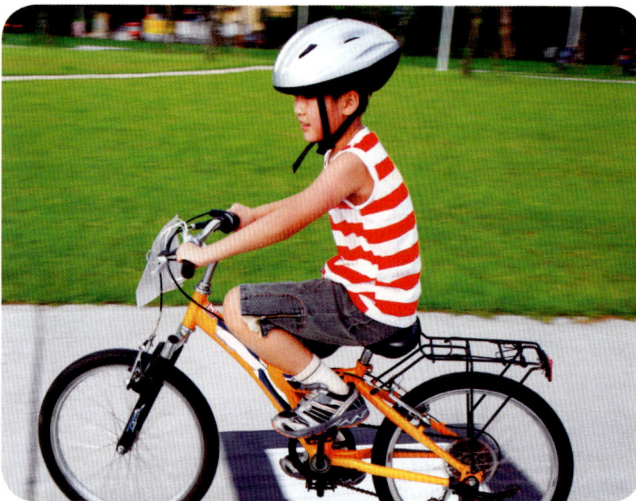

Wearing a helmet

Writing

4. Avoid drinking alcohol, taking drugs, and smoking; they are very harmful for your nervous system

5. Give a workout to your brain by doing challenging activities, such as puzzles, reading, playing music, making art, or even writing

6. Get enough rest and try to have at least eight hours of sleep at night

7. Learn to relax and reduce stress by practicing deep breathing exercises, doing yoga or meditation

8. Surround yourself with positive people who will make you feel good about yourself

9. Train your brain not to pay attention to negative thoughts

One of the best ways of keeping your nervous system fine tuned is to spend a minimum of 15 minutes per day writing on paper as neatly as you can.

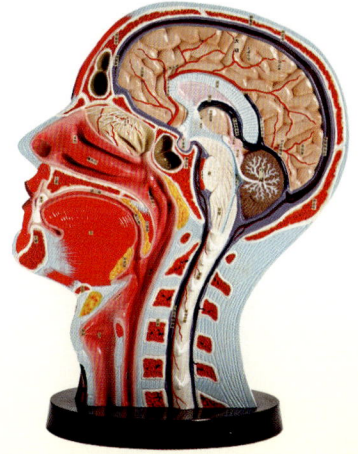

Test Your
MEMORY

1. What is the study of nervous system called?

2. What are nerves?

3. What are the two parts of the nervous system?

4. What are the two parts of the Peripheral Nervous System?

5. Nervous system is made up of which two categories of cells?

6. Name the three main parts of a neuron.

7. Name the two types of neurons.

8. What is the weight of brain of an average adult human being?

9. What is the length of the spinal cord in men and women?

10. Name the five major parts of the brain.

11. Which part of our brain controls balance, movement and coordination of our muscles?

12. How many vertebrae humans have in their necks?

Index

A

Alzheimer's disease 22
amygdale 10
aura 23
Autonomic Nervous System
    5, 15, 16
axon 6, 7, 8, 19

B

Bell's Palsy 21
Brain stem 11, 12

C

Central Nervous System 5, 7,
    8, 9, 10, 15, 18, 19, 20
Cerebellum 9, 11, 12, 13
Cerebral palsy 18
Cerebrum 9, 11, 12, 13

D

dendrites 6, 7

E

Epilepsy 18, 27

G

glands 8, 16
glial cells 6, 7

H

Hypothalamus 9, 11, 12

I

interneurons 7
involuntary nervous system
    16

M

motor neurons 7, 8, 13
Multiple Sclerosis 19
myelin 6, 7, 19

N

nerve fibres 6, 13
nerve roots 13
nerves 3, 4, 6, 7, 8, 9, 10,
    12, 13, 15, 17
nerve tissue 7, 13
neurologist 18
neurons 4, 5, 6, 7, 8, 9, 13, 14
neurotransmitter chemicals
    8

P

Parasympathetic Nervous
    System 16, 17
Parkinson's disease 20

Peripheral Nervous System
    5, 7, 9, 13, 15, 16, 18
Pituitary gland 9, 11, 12

R

reflex 14

S

seizures 23, 24, 25, 26, 27
Sensory neurons 7, 14
Somatic Nervous System 5,
    15
spinal cord 3, 5, 7, 8, 9, 10,
    11, 12, 13, 14, 15, 18, 19
Sympathetic Nervous Sys-
    tem 5, 16, 17

T

tissue 4, 7, 8, 13

W

wine and dine 17